Bob Dylan
for ukulele

**Twenty-three Bob Dylan classics arranged for ukulele!
Complete with full lyrics and easy-to-read chord boxes.**

EXCLUSIVELY DISTRIBUTED BY

HAL•LEONARD®

Cover photo: Ken Regan/Camera 5
Project editor: David Bradley

This book Copyright © 2010 Special Rider Music

This book published 2010 by Amsco Publications,

Order No. AM1000549
International Standard Book Number: 978-0-8256-3744-5
HL Item Number: 14037684

Exclusive Distributor for the United States, Canada, Mexico and U.S. possessions:
Hal Leonard Corporation
7777 West Bluemound Road, Milwaukee, WI 53213 USA

ALL ALONG THE WATCHTOWER
Words and Music by Bob Dylan

C#m   C#m/B   A   B   C#

Moderately, with a beat

C#m   C#m/B   A   B
"There must be some way   out   of here,"

C#m   C#m/B   A   B
said the jok - er to the thief

C#m   C#m/B   A   B
"There's too much con - fu - sion,

C#m   C#m/B   A   B
I can't get no re - lief

C#m   C#m/B   A   B
Bus - 'ness men, they drink my wine,

C#m   C#m/B   A   B
plow - men dig my earth

C#m   C#m/B   A   B
None of them a - long the line

C#m   C#m/B   A   B
know what an - y of it is worth"

C#m   C#m/B   A   B
"No rea - son to get ex - cit - ed,"

C#m   C#m/B   A   B
the thief, he kind - ly spoke

C#m   C#m/B   A   B
"There are man - y here a - mong us

C#m   C#m/B   A   B
who feel that life is but a joke

C#m			C#m/B			A			B		

But you and I, we've been through that,

C#m			C#m/B			A			B		

and this is not our fate

C#m			C#m/B			A			B		

So let us not talk false - ly now,

C#m			C#m/B			A			B		

the hour is get - ting late"

C#m			C#m/B			A			B		

All a - long the watch - tow - er,

C#m			C#m/B			A			B		

prin - ces kept the view

C#m			C#m/B			A			B		

While all the wom - en came and went,

C#m			C#m/B			A			B		

bare - foot ser - vants, too

C#m			C#m/B			A			B		

Out - side in the dis - tance

C#m			C#m/B			A			B		

a wild - cat did growl

C#m			C#m/B			A			B		

Two rid - ers were ap - proach - ing,

C#m			C#m/B			A			B		C#

the wind be - gan to howl

ALL I REALLY WANT TO DO
Words and Music by Bob Dylan

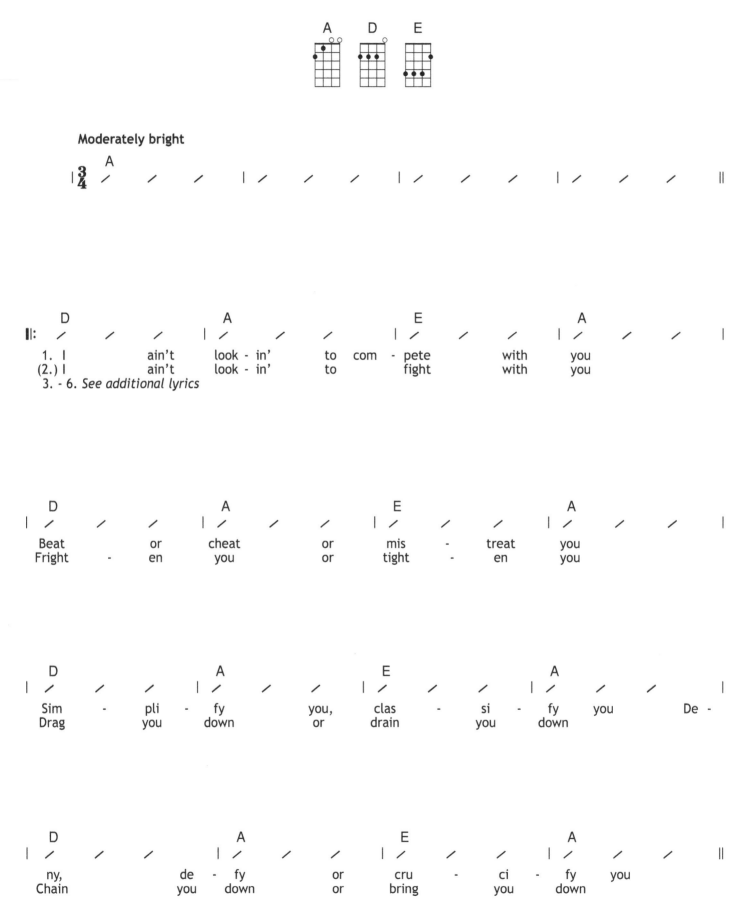

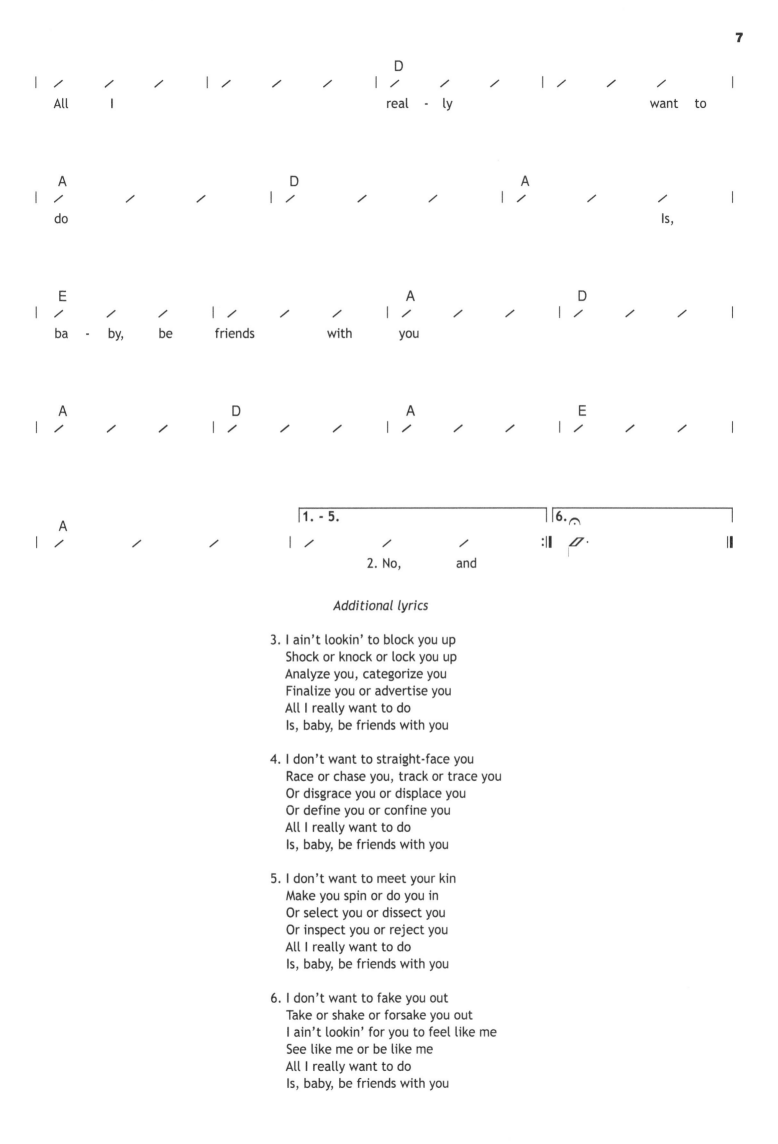

| | | | | | | | D | | | | | | |
All   I   real - ly   want to

A   D   A
do   Is,

E   A   D
ba - by,   be   friends   with   you

A   D   A   E

A
                                    | 1. - 5. | | 6. |
                                    2. No,   and

Additional lyrics

3. I ain't lookin' to block you up
   Shock or knock or lock you up
   Analyze you, categorize you
   Finalize you or advertise you
   All I really want to do
   Is, baby, be friends with you

4. I don't want to straight-face you
   Race or chase you, track or trace you
   Or disgrace you or displace you
   Or define you or confine you
   All I really want to do
   Is, baby, be friends with you

5. I don't want to meet your kin
   Make you spin or do you in
   Or select you or dissect you
   Or inspect you or reject you
   All I really want to do
   Is, baby, be friends with you

6. I don't want to fake you out
   Take or shake or forsake you out
   I ain't lookin' for you to feel like me
   See like me or be like me
   All I really want to do
   Is, baby, be friends with you

BEYOND HERE LIES NOTHIN'
Music by Bob Dylan. Lyrics by Bob Dylan with Robert Hunter.

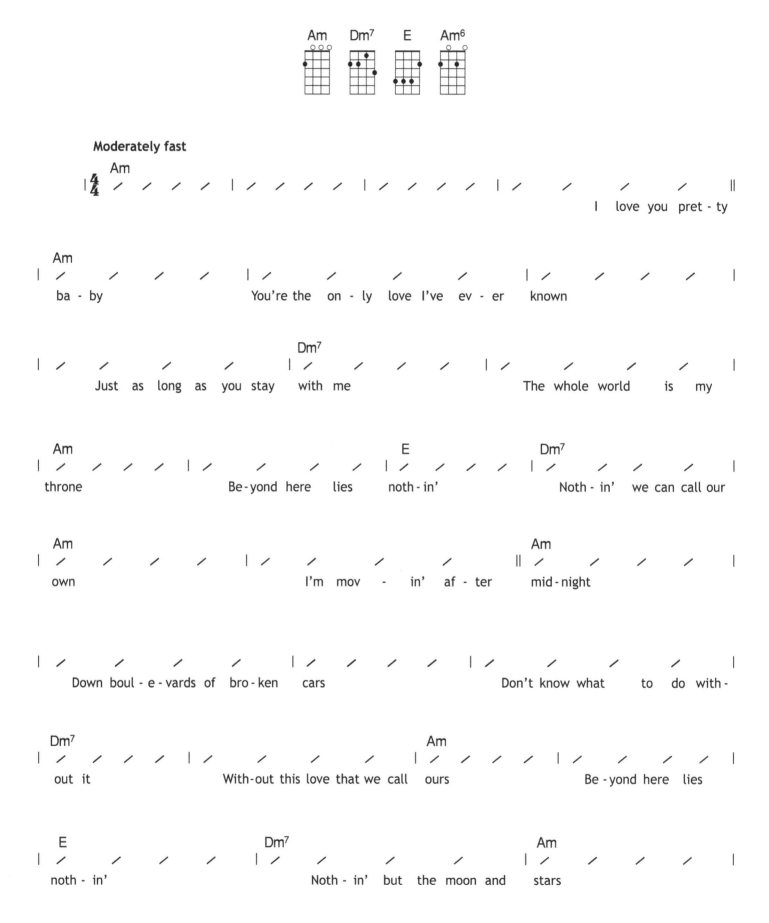

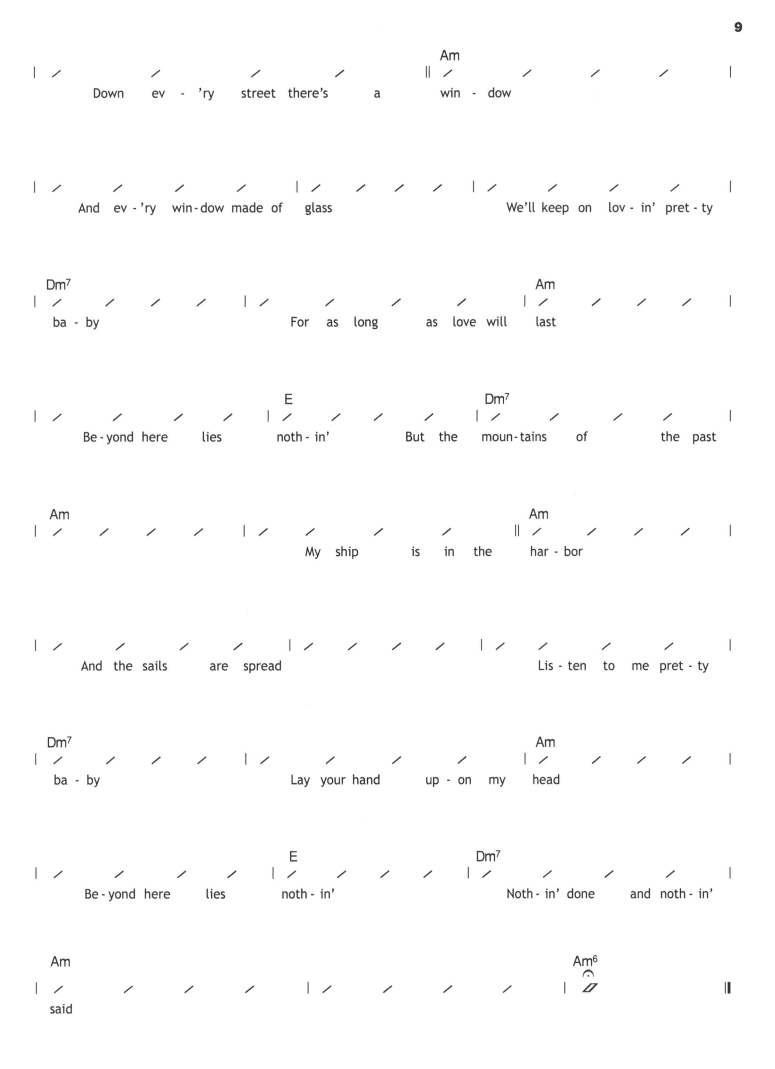

BEYOND THE HORIZON
Words and Music by Bob Dylan

F   Fmaj7   Eb9   F#dim7   C7   Bb   Bbm   G7

Moderately, with a swing

F   Fmaj7   Eb9
1. Be -yond the ho - ri - zon,   be - hind the sun
2. - 4. *See additional lyrics*

F   F#dim7   C7/G   F#dim7   C7/G
At   the   end   of   the   rain - bow

C7   F   Fmaj7
life has on - ly be - gun   In   the   long hours of twi -

F   Fmaj7   Eb9   F   F#dim7
- light   'neath the star - dust a - bove

C7/G   F#dim7   C7/G   C7
Be -yond the ho - ri - zon   it   is   eas - y to love

F   Bb   Bbm   F
My   wretch - ed   heart's pound - ing

C7   F   Bb   Bbm
I felt an an - gel's kiss   My mem -'ries are drown -

F   G7   C7
ing   In mor - tal bliss   Be - yond the ho - ri -

F   Fmaj7   Eb9   F   F#dim7
- zon   In   the   Spring-time or Fall

C⁷/G		F#dim⁷		C⁷/G				C⁷				

Love waits for - ev - er   for one and for all

F N.C.				**1.**				**2., 3.**		F	Fmaj⁷	

2. Be - yond the ho - ri -

E♭9				F		F#dim⁷ C⁷/G	F#dim⁷	C⁷/G		C⁷		

F N.C.				**4.**				F	

3., 4. Be - yond the ho - ri -   *rit.*

Additional lyrics

2. Beyond the horizon across the divide
  'Round about midnight, we'll be on the same side
  Down in the valley the water runs cold
  Beyond the horizon someone prayed for your soul

  I'm touched with desire
  What don't I do?
  I'll throw the logs on the fire
  I'll build my world around you

  Beyond the horizon, at the end of the game
  Every step that you take, I'm walking the same

3. Beyond the horizon the night winds blow
  The theme of a melody from many moons ago
  The bells of St. Mary, how sweetly they chime
  Beyond the horizon I found you just in time

  It's dark and it's dreary
  I ponder in vain
  I'm weakened, I'm weary
  My repentance is plain

  Beyond the horizon o'r the treacherous sea
  I still can't believe that you've set aside your love for me

4. Beyond the horizon, 'neath crimson skies
  In the soft light of morning I'll follow you with my eyes
  Through countries and kingdoms and temples of stone
  Beyond the horizon right down to the bone

  It's late in the season
  Never knew, never cared
  Whatever the reason
  Someone's life has been spared

  Beyond the horizon the sky is so blue
  I've got more than a lifetime to live lovin' you

BLOWIN' IN THE WIND
Words and Music by Bob Dylan

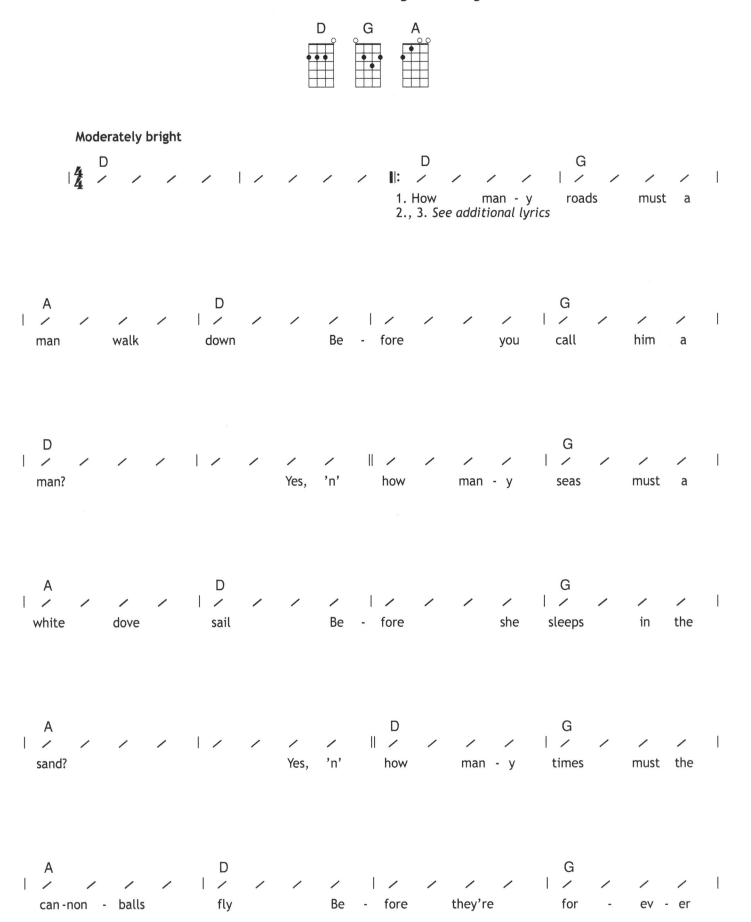

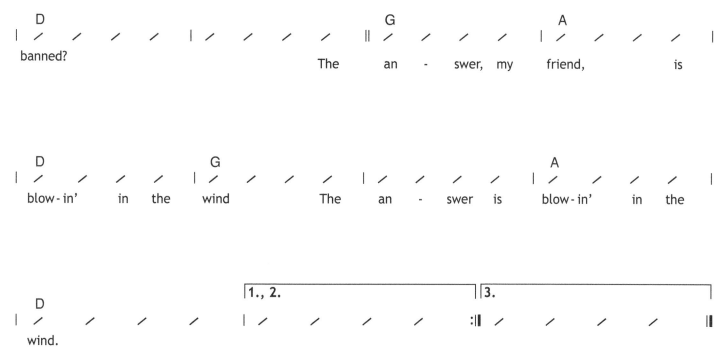

D

banned?

G

The an - swer, my friend, is

A

D

blow-in' in the wind

G

The an - swer is blow-in' in the

A

D

wind.

1., 2.

3.

Additional lyrics

2. How many years can a mountain exist
   Before it's washed to the sea?
   Yes, 'n' how many years can some people exist
   Before they're allowed to be free?
   Yes, 'n' how many times can a man turn his head
   Pretending he just doesn't see?
   The answer, my friend, is blowin' in the wind
   The answer is blowin' in the wind

3. How many times must a man look up
   Before he can see the sky?
   Yes, 'n' how many ears must one man have
   Before he can hear people cry?
   Yes, 'n' how many deaths will it take till he knows
   That too many people have died?
   The answer, my friend, is blowin' in the wind
   The answer is blowin' in the wind

DON'T THINK TWICE, IT'S ALL RIGHT

Words and Music by Bob Dylan

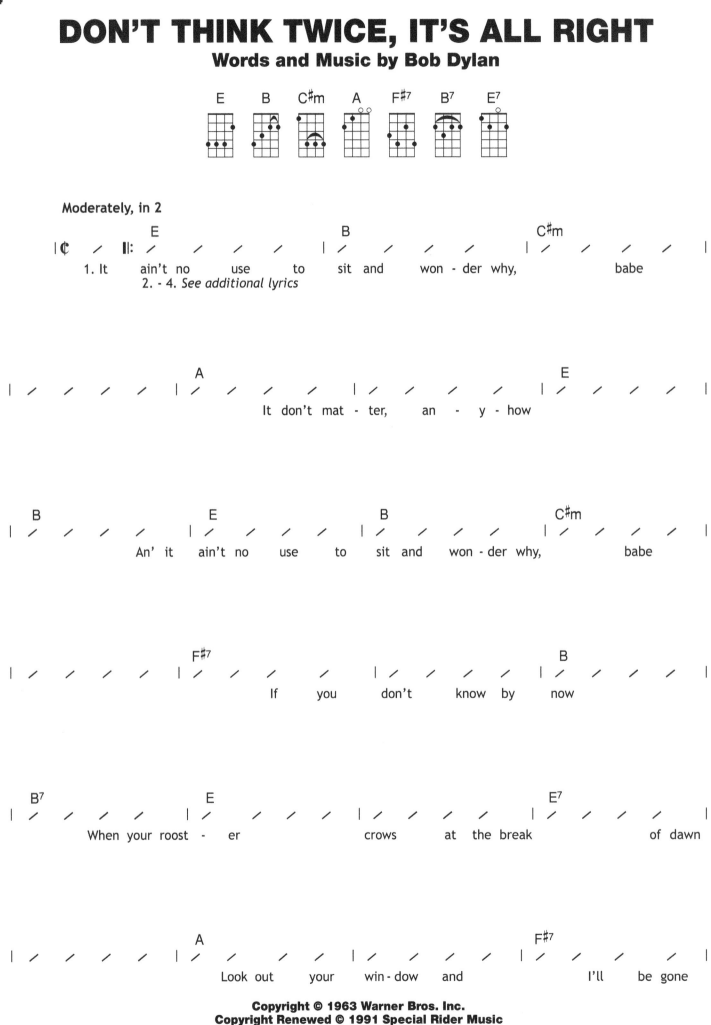

Moderately, in 2

1. It ain't no use to sit and won - der why, babe
2. - 4. *See additional lyrics*

It don't mat - ter, an - y - how

An' it ain't no use to sit and won - der why, babe

If you don't know by now

When your roost - er crows at the break of dawn

Look out your win - dow and I'll be gone

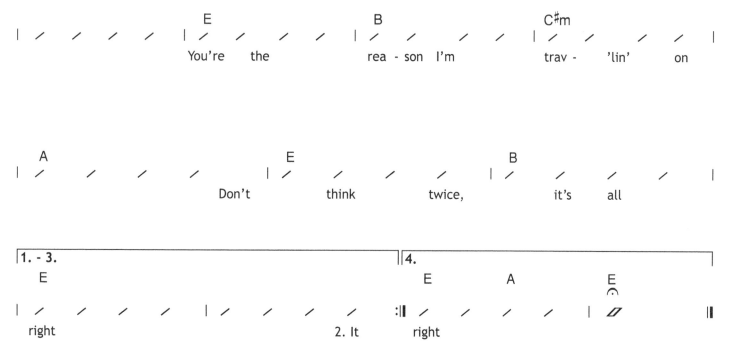

E	B	C#m

You're the rea - son I'm trav - 'lin' on

A	E	B

Don't think twice, it's all

1. - 3.

E

right

2. It

4.

E   A   E

right

Additional lyrics

2. It ain't no use in turnin' on your light, babe
   That light I never knowed
   An' it ain't no use in turnin' on your light, babe
   I'm on the dark side of the road
   Still I wish there was somethin' you would do or say
   To try and make me change my mind and stay
   We never did too much talkin' anyway
   So don't think twice, it's all right

3. It ain't no use in callin' out my name, gal
   Like you never did before
   It ain't no use in callin' out my name, gal
   I can't hear you anymore
   I'm a-thinkin' and a-wond'rin' all the way down the road
   I once loved a woman, a child I'm told
   I gave her my heart but she wanted my soul
   But don't think twice, it's all right

4. I'm walkin' down that long, lonesome road, babe
   Where I'm bound, I can't tell
   But goodbye's too good a word, gal
   So I'll just say fare thee well
   I ain't sayin' you treated me unkind
   You could have done better but I don't mind
   You just kinda wasted my precious time
   But don't think twice, it's all right

FOREVER YOUNG

Words and Music by Bob Dylan

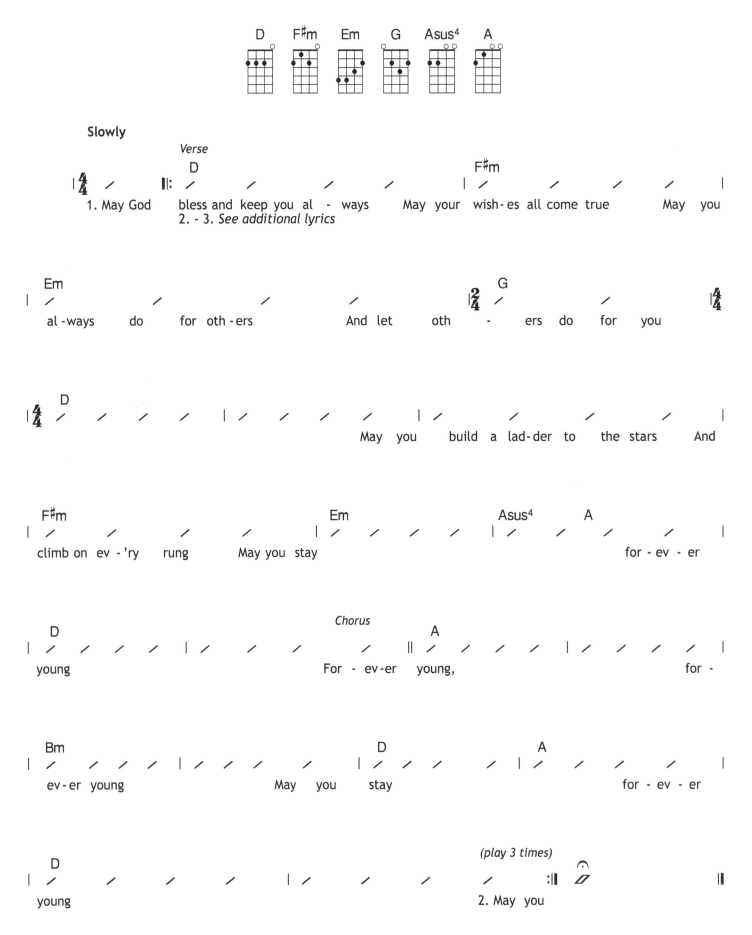

Additional lyrics

2. May you grow up to be righteous
   May you grow up to be true
   May you always know the truth
   And see the lights surrounding you
   May you always be courageous
   Stand upright and be strong
   May you stay forever young

Chorus
   Forever young, forever young
   May you stay forever young

3. May your hands always be busy
   May your feet always be swift
   May you have a strong foundation
   When the winds of changes shift
   May your heart always be joyful
   May your song always be sung
   May you stay forever young

Chorus
   Forever young, forever young
   May you stay forever young

I FEEL A CHANGE COMIN' ON
Music by Bob Dylan. Lyrics by Bob Dylan with Robert Hunter.

F⁷sus⁴ B♭ Gm⁷ Cm⁷ F⁷ E♭ B♭⁷ C⁷ F

Moderately

Intro

F⁷sus⁴ / / / / | / / / / | / / / / |
B♭

Well I'm

B♭ / / / / Gm⁷ / / | Cm⁷ / / / F⁷ / / | B♭ / / / Gm⁷ / / |
look-ing the world o-ver   Look-ing far off in-to the East

Cm⁷ / F⁷ / / | B♭ / / / | Gm⁷ / / Cm⁷ / / F⁷ / / / |
And I see my ba-by com-ing   She's walk-ing with the vil-lage priest

B♭ / / Gm⁷ / / Cm⁷ / / F⁷ / / | / B♭ / / Gm⁷ / / |
I feel a change com-ing on   And the

F⁷sus⁴ / / / / / | / B♭ / E♭ / | / B♭ / F / / |
last part of the day is al - read-y gone   We got

B♭ / / Gm⁷ / / Cm⁷ / / F⁷ / / | B♭ / / Gm⁷ / / |
so much in com-mon   We strive for the same old ends

Cm⁷ / / F⁷ / / | B♭ / / Gm⁷ / / Cm⁷ / / F⁷ / / |
And I just can't wait   Wait for us to be-come

B♭ / / Gm⁷ / / Cm⁷ / / F⁷ / / | B♭ / / Gm⁷ / / |
friends   I feel a change com-ing on   And the

F⁷sus⁴ / / / / / | / B♭ / E♭ / | / B♭ / F / / |
fourth part of the day is al - read-y gone

Bb		Gm7		Cm7		F7		Bb		Gm7	

Life is for love   And they say that love is blind

Cm7		F7		Bb		Gm7		Cm7		F7	

If you want to live eas - y   Ba - by pack your clothes with

Bb		Gm7		Cm7		F7		Bb		Gm7	

mine   I feel a change com-ing on   And the

F7sus4						Bb		Eb		Bb		Bb7

fourth part of the day is al - read-y gone   Well now

‖: | Eb | | | | | | | | | Bb | | | |
|---|---|---|---|---|---|---|---|---|---|---|---|---|

(1.) what's the use in dream - in'   You got bet - ter things to do
(2.) Bil - ly Joe Shav - er   And I'm read - ing James Joyce

		Bb7		Eb									

Dreams nev - er did work for me an - y way
Some peo - ple they tell me I got the

𝄋 *Instrumental solo on D.S. (fade)*

C7						F			‖ Bb		Gm7	

E - ven when they did come true   You are as whor-ish as ev - er
blood of the land in my voice   Ev -'ry-bod - y got all the mon-ey

Cm7		F7		Bb	Gm7		Cm7		F7		

Ba - by you could start a fire   I must be los -
Ev -'ry-bod-y got all the beau-ti-ful clothes   Ev -'ry-bod-y got

Bb		Gm7		Cm7		F7		Bb		Gm7	

- ing my mind   You're the ob - ject of my de - sire }
all the flow - ers   I don't have one sin - gle rose }

Cm7		F7				Bb		Gm7			

I feel a change com - ing on   And the

|1.‾‾‾‾‾‾‾‾‾‾‾‾‾‾‾‾‾‾‾‾‾‾‾| |2. *D.S. and fade*|

F7sus4					Bb	Eb	Bb		Bb7	:‖ Bb	F	

fourth part of the day is al - read-y gone   2. I'm lis-ten-ing to

I WANT YOU

Words and Music by Bob Dylan

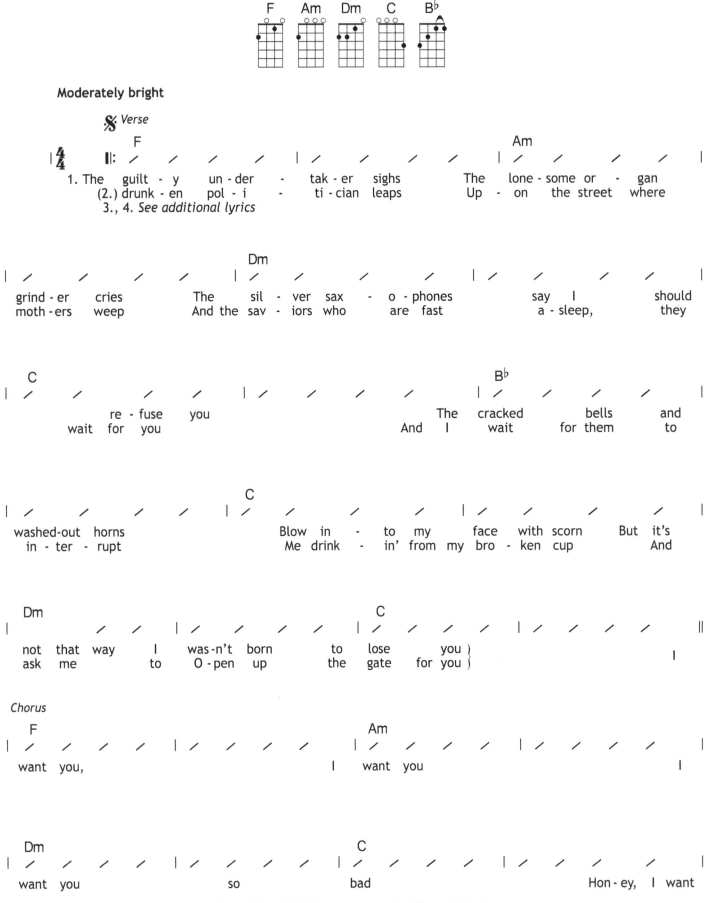

Moderately bright

Verse

F   Am

1. The guilt-y un-der-tak-er sighs   The lone-some or-gan
(2.) drunk-en pol-i-ti-cian leaps   Up-on the street where
3., 4. *See additional lyrics*

                              Dm

grind-er cries   The sil-ver sax-o-phones   say I   should
moth-ers weep   And the sav-iors who   are fast   a-sleep,   they

C   Bb

re-fuse you   The cracked   bells   and
wait for you   And I   wait   for them   to

                              C

washed-out horns   Blow in-to my   face with scorn   But it's
in-ter-rupt   Me drink-in' from my   bro-ken cup   And

Dm   C

not that way   I was-n't born   to lose   you)
ask me   to O-pen up   the gate   for you)

Chorus

F   Am

want you,   I want you

Dm   C

want you   so   bad   Hon-ey, I want

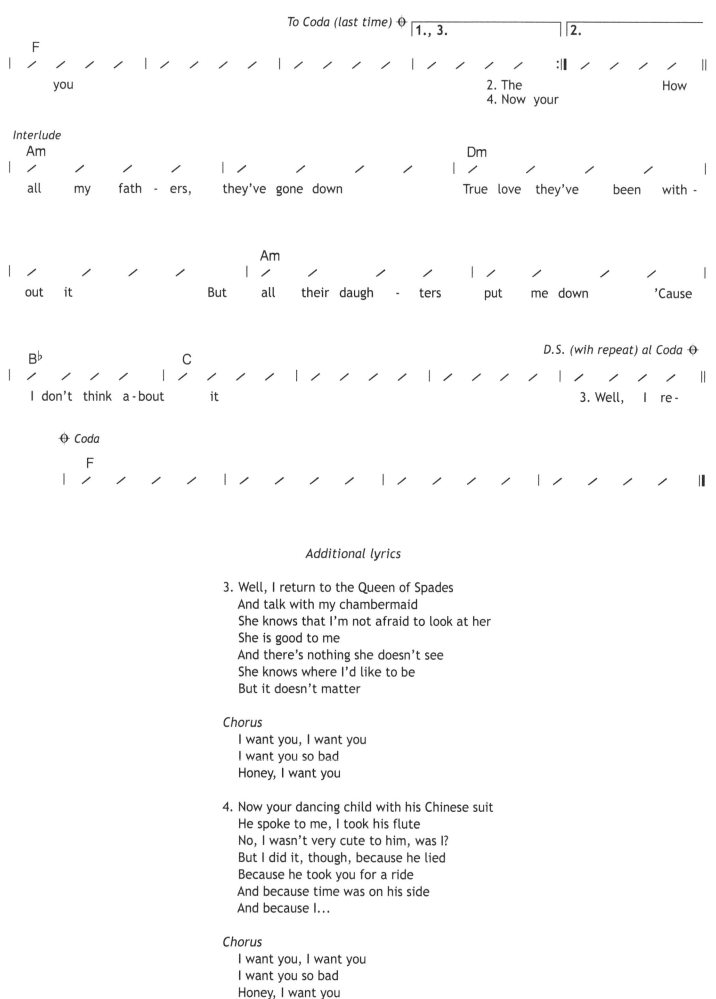

To Coda (last time) ⊕

|1., 3. | |2. |

F

you

2. The   How
4. Now your

Interlude

Am   Dm

all   my   fath - ers,   they've gone down   True love they've   been   with -

Am

out   it   But   all   their daugh - ters   put   me   down   'Cause

B♭   C   *D.S. (wih repeat) al Coda* ⊕

I don't think a-bout   it   3. Well,   I re -

⊕ *Coda*

F

Additional lyrics

3. Well, I return to the Queen of Spades
   And talk with my chambermaid
   She knows that I'm not afraid to look at her
   She is good to me
   And there's nothing she doesn't see
   She knows where I'd like to be
   But it doesn't matter

Chorus
   I want you, I want you
   I want you so bad
   Honey, I want you

4. Now your dancing child with his Chinese suit
   He spoke to me, I took his flute
   No, I wasn't very cute to him, was I?
   But I did it, though, because he lied
   Because he took you for a ride
   And because time was on his side
   And because I...

Chorus
   I want you, I want you
   I want you so bad
   Honey, I want you

I'LL BE YOUR BABY TONIGHT
Words and Music by Bob Dylan

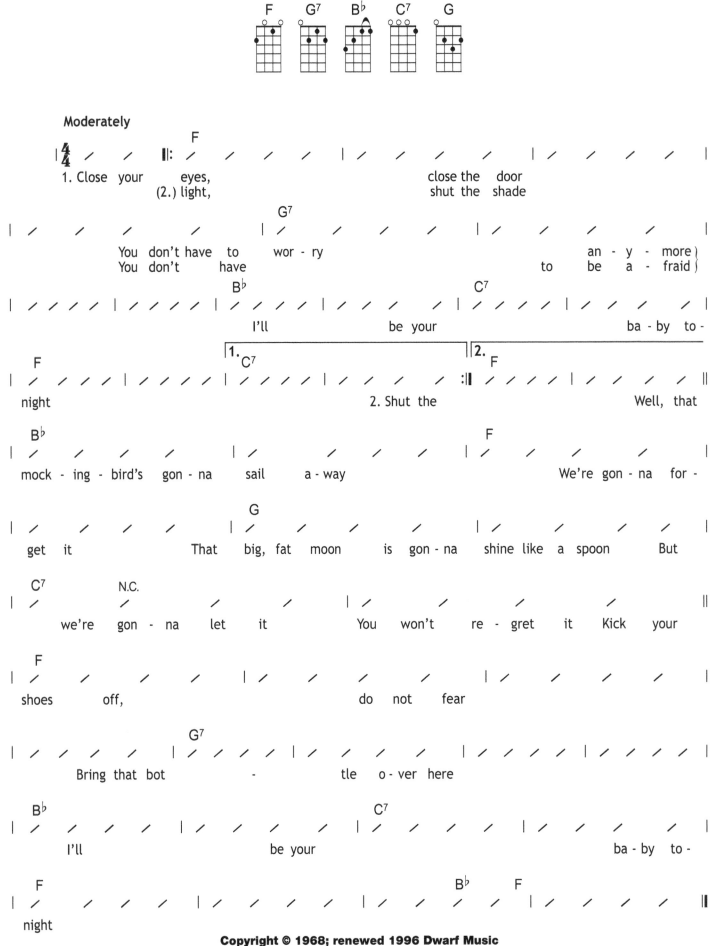

QUINN THE ESKIMO (THE MIGHTY QUINN)

Words and Music by Bob Dylan

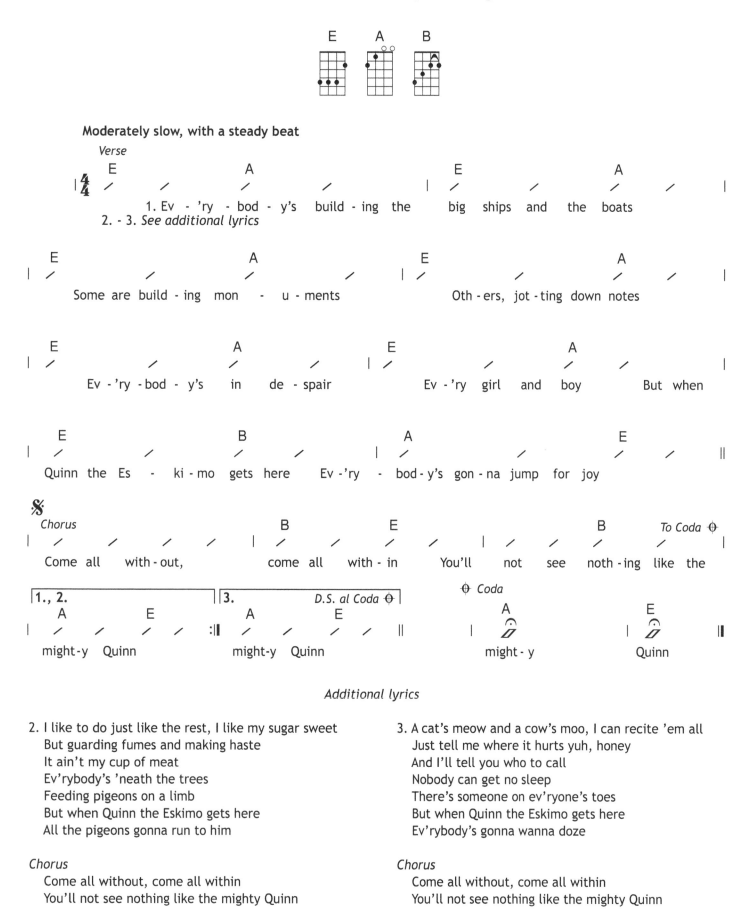

Moderately slow, with a steady beat

Verse

1. Ev - 'ry - bod - y's build - ing the big ships and the boats

2. - 3. *See additional lyrics*

Some are build - ing mon - u - ments   Oth - ers, jot - ting down notes

Ev - 'ry - bod - y's in de - spair   Ev - 'ry girl and boy   But when

Quinn the Es - ki - mo gets here   Ev - 'ry - bod - y's gon - na jump for joy

Chorus

Come all with - out,   come all with - in   You'll not see noth - ing like the

To Coda

1., 2.   might - y Quinn

3.   *D.S. al Coda*   might - y Quinn

Coda   might - y   Quinn

Additional lyrics

2. I like to do just like the rest, I like my sugar sweet
But guarding fumes and making haste
It ain't my cup of meat
Ev'rybody's 'neath the trees
Feeding pigeons on a limb
But when Quinn the Eskimo gets here
All the pigeons gonna run to him

Chorus
Come all without, come all within
You'll not see nothing like the mighty Quinn

3. A cat's meow and a cow's moo, I can recite 'em all
Just tell me where it hurts yuh, honey
And I'll tell you who to call
Nobody can get no sleep
There's someone on ev'ryone's toes
But when Quinn the Eskimo gets here
Ev'rybody's gonna wanna doze

Chorus
Come all without, come all within
You'll not see nothing like the mighty Quinn

IT AIN'T ME, BABE
Words and Music by Bob Dylan

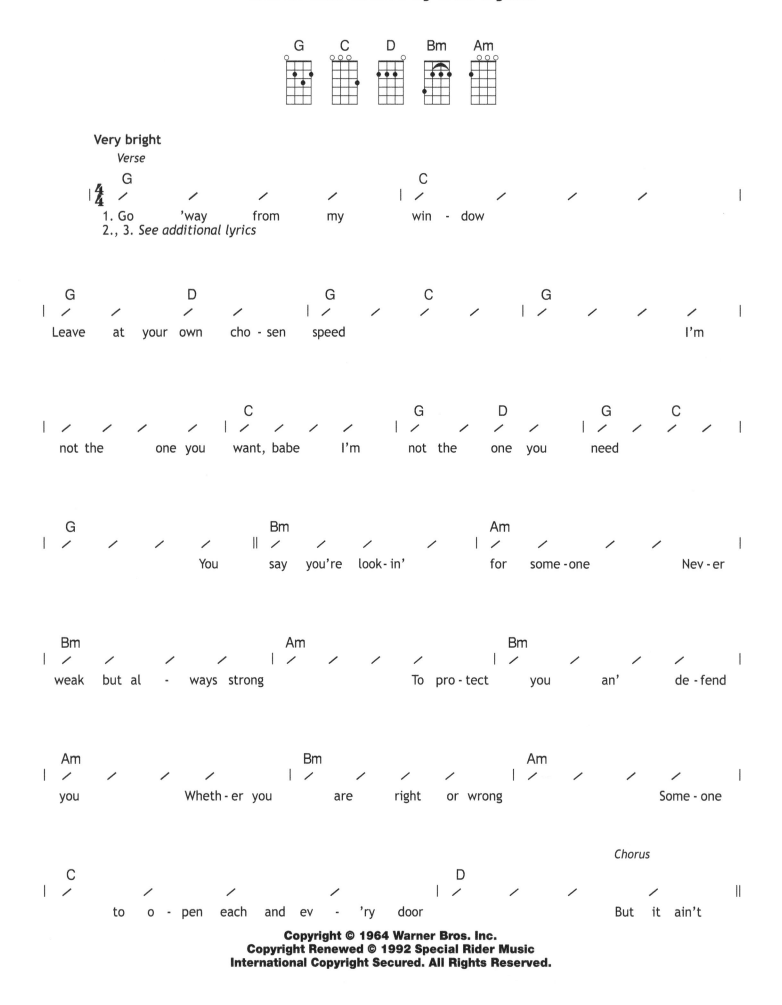

Very bright

Verse

G
4/4 1. Go   'way   from   my   win - dow
     2., 3. *See additional lyrics*

C

G   D   G   C   G
Leave   at   your   own   cho - sen   speed   I'm

C   G   D   G   C
not the   one you   want, babe   I'm   not the   one you   need

G   Bm   Am
You   say   you're   look-in'   for   some-one   Nev-er

Bm   Am   Bm
weak   but   al - ways   strong   To pro-tect   you   an'   de-fend

Am   Bm   Am
you   Wheth-er you   are   right   or wrong   Some-one

Chorus

C   D
to o-pen   each   and ev - 'ry   door   But   it   ain't

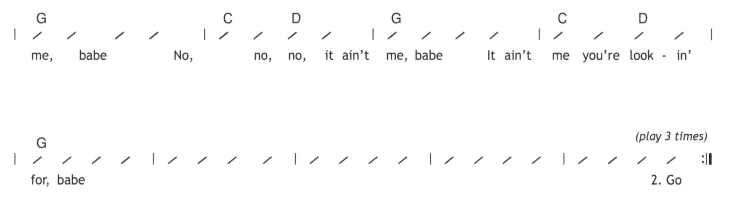

G				C	D			G				C		D	
me,	babe		No,		no,	no,	it ain't	me, babe				It ain't	me	you're	look - in'

(play 3 times)

for, babe   2. Go

Additional lyrics

2. Go lightly from the ledge, babe
   Go lightly on the ground
   I'm not the one you want, babe
   I will only let you down
   You say you're lookin' for someone
   Who will promise never to part
   Someone to close his eyes for you
   Someone to close his heart
   Someone who will die for you an' more

Chorus
   But it ain't me, babe
   No, no, no, it ain't me, babe
   It ain't me you're lookin' for, babe

3. Go melt back into the night, babe
   Everything inside is made of stone
   There's nothing in here moving
   An' anyway I'm not alone
   You say you're lookin' for someone
   Who'll pick you up each time you fall
   To gather flowers constantly
   An' to come each time you call
   A lover for your life an' nothing more

Chorus
   But it ain't me, babe
   No, no, no, it ain't me, babe
   It ain't me you're lookin' for, babe

IT'S ALL OVER NOW, BABY BLUE

Words and Music by Bob Dylan

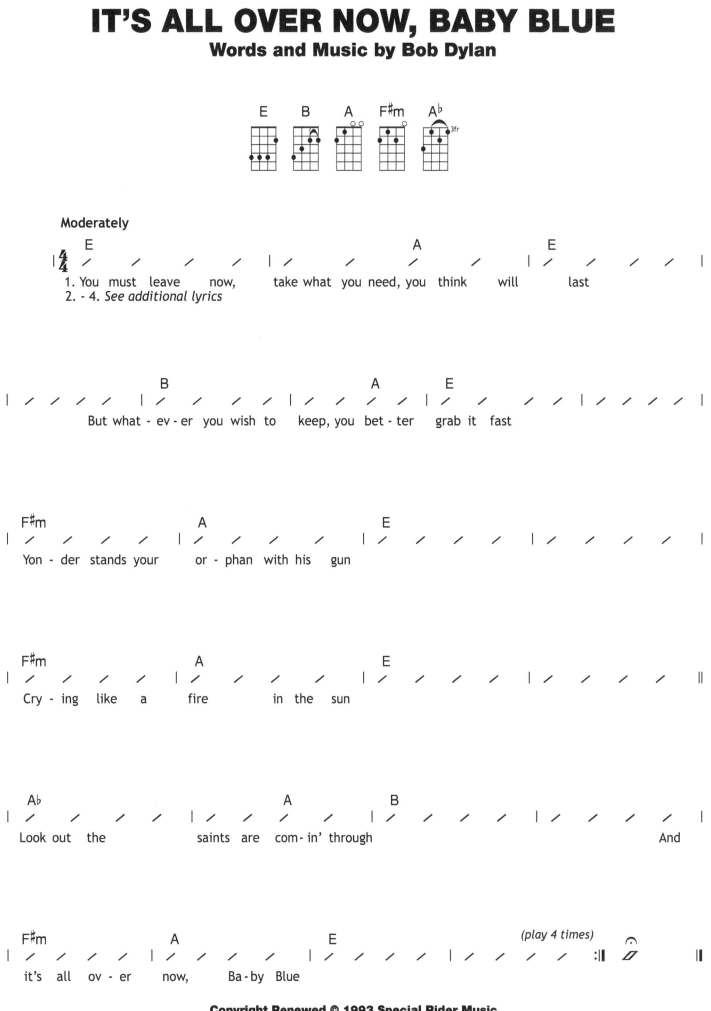

E   B   A   F#m   Ab

Moderately

E   A   E

1. You must leave now,   take what you need, you think   will   last
2. - 4. *See additional lyrics*

B   A   E

But what - ev - er you wish to   keep, you bet - ter   grab it fast

F#m   A   E

Yon - der stands your   or - phan with his   gun

F#m   A   E

Cry - ing like a   fire   in the   sun

Ab   A   B

Look out the   saints are com - in' through   And

(play 4 times)

F#m   A   E

it's all ov - er   now,   Ba - by Blue

Additional lyrics

2. The highway is for gamblers, better use your sense
   Take what you have gathered from coincidence
   The empty-handed painter from your streets
   Is drawing crazy patterns on your sheets
   This sky, too, is folding under you
   And it's all over now, Baby Blue

3. All your seasick sailors, they are rowing home
   All your reindeer armies, are all going home
   The lover who just walked out your door
   Has taken all his blankets from the floor
   The carpet, too, is moving under you
   And it's all over now, Baby Blue

4. Leave your stepping stones behind, something calls for you
   Forget the dead you've left, they will not follow you
   The vagabond who's rapping at your door
   Is standing in the clothes that you once wore
   Strike another match, go start anew
   And it's all over now, Baby Blue

KNOCKIN' ON HEAVEN'S DOOR

Words and Music by Bob Dylan

Chorus

| G | | | D | | | Am⁷ | | | | |
Knock, knock, knock - in' on heav - en's door

| G | | | D | | | C | | | | |
Knock, knock, knock - in' on heav - en's door

| G | | | D | | | Am⁷ | | | | |
Knock, knock, knock - in' on heav - en's door

1.

| G | | | D | | | C | | | | :||
Knock, knock, knock - in' on heav - en's door

2.

(repeat to fade)

| C | | | | ||: | G | D | Am⁷ | | | | G | D | C | | | :||
Ooh   Ooh

LAY, LADY, LAY
Words and Music by Bob Dylan

A   C#m   G   Bm   E   F#m   D

Slowly

| A | | C#m | | G | | Bm | | A | C#m |
Lay, la - dy, lay,   lay a-cross my big brass bed

| G | Bm | | A | | C#m | | G | | Bm |
Lay, la - dy, lay,   lay a-cross my big brass bed

| A | C#m | | G | Bm | | E | | F#m |
What - ev - er col - ors you have

| A | | | E | | F#m |
in your mind   I'll show them to you

| A | | | | C#m |
and you'll see them shine   Lay, la - dy, lay,

| G | Bm | | A | C#m | G | Bm |
lay a - cross my big brass bed

| A | C#m | | G | | Bm |
Stay, la - dy, stay,   stay with your man a - while

| A | C#m | | G | Bm | | A | | C#m |
Un - til the break of day,

| G | Bm | | A | C#m | G | Bm |
let me see you make him smile

| E | | F#m | | A |
His clothes are dirt - y but his   hands are clean

E   F#m   A

And you're the   best   thing   that he's   ev - er   seen

C#m   G   Bm

Stay, la - dy, stay,   stay with your man   a - while

A   C#m   G   Bm   C#m

Why wait an - y long - er for   the

E F#m   A   C#m   Bm

world to be - gin   You can have your cake   and eat it too

A   C#m

Why   wait an - y long - er for   the

E F#m   A   C#m

one you love   When he's stand - ing   in front of

Bm   A   C#m   G   Bm

you   Lay, la - dy, lay,   lay a-cross my big brass bed

A   C#m   G   Bm   A   C#m

Stay, la - dy, stay,

G   Bm   A   C#m   G   Bm

stay while the night   is   still a - head

E   F#m   A   E   F#m

I long to see you in the morn - ing light   I long to reach for you

A   C#m

in   the   night   Stay, la - dy, stay,

G   Bm   A   C#m

stay while the night   is   still a - head

G   Bm   A   Bm   C#m   D   A

LIKE A ROLLING STONE
Words and Music by Bob Dylan

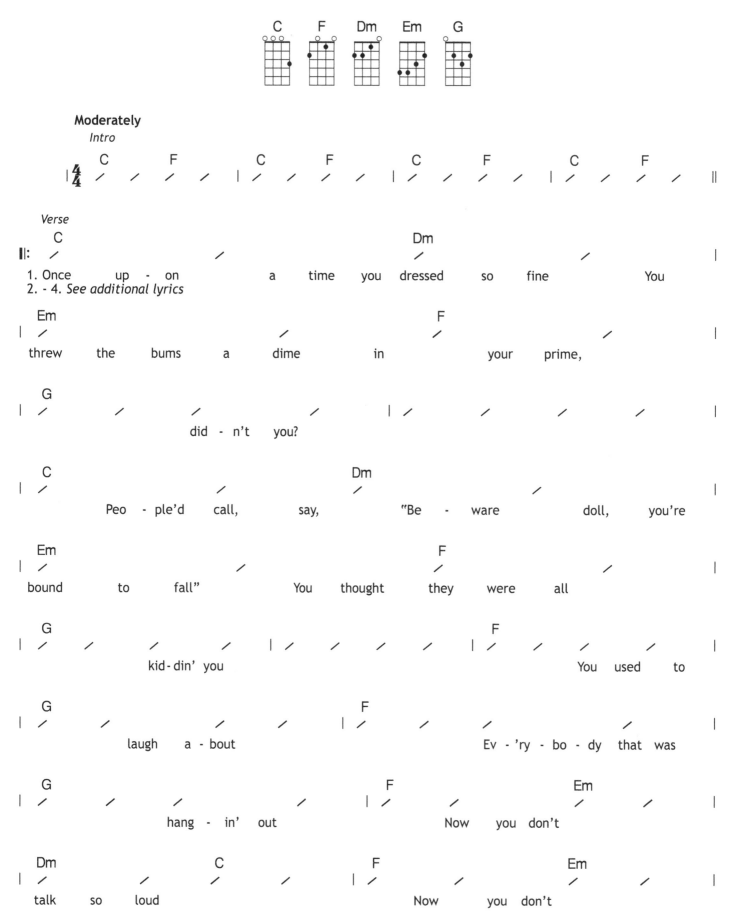

Moderately

Intro

| C | F | C | F | C | F | C | F |

Verse

C ... Dm
1. Once up - on a time you dressed so fine You
2. - 4. *See additional lyrics*

Em ... F
threw the bums a dime in your prime,

G
did - n't you?

C ... Dm
Peo - ple'd call, say, "Be - ware doll, you're

Em ... F
bound to fall" You thought they were all

G ... F
kid - din' you You used to

G ... F
laugh a - bout Ev - 'ry - bo - dy that was

G ... F ... Em
hang - in' out Now you don't

Dm ... C ... F ... Em
talk so loud Now you don't

Dm   C   Dm

| ╱   ╱   ╱   ╱ | ╱   ╱   ╱   ╱ |

seem   so   proud   A - bout   hav - ing   to   be   scroung - ing

F   G   *Chorus*

| ╱   ╱   ╱   ╱ | ╱   ╱   ╱   ╱ | ╱   ╱   ╱   ╱ ‖

for   your   next   meal   How   does   it   feel

C   F   G   C   F   G

| ╱ ╱ ╱ ╱ | ╱ ╱ ╱ ╱ | ╱ ╱ ╱ ╱ | ╱ ╱ ╱ ╱ |

How   does   it   feel   To   be   with - out   a   home

C   F   G

| ╱   ╱   ╱   ╱ | ╱   ╱   ╱   ╱ |

Like   a   com - plete   un -

C   F   G   C   F   G

| ╱ ╱ ╱ ╱ | ╱ ╱ ╱ ╱ | ╱ ╱ ╱ ╱ | ╱ ╱ ╱ ╱ |

known   Like   a   roll - ing   stone?

C   F   G   *(play 4 times)*

| ╱ ╱ ╱ ╱ | ╱ ╱ ╱ ╱ | ╱ ╱ ╱ ╱ :‖

C   F   G   *(repeat and fade)*

‖: ╱   ╱   ╱   ╱ | ╱   ╱   ╱   ╱ :‖

Additional lyrics

2. You've gone to the finest school all right, Miss Loney
   But you know you only used to get juiced in it
   And nobody has ever taught you how to live on the street
   And now you find out you're gonna have to get used to it
   You said you'd never compromise
   With the mystery tramp, but now you realize
   He's not selling any alibis
   As you stare into the vacuum of his eyes
   And ask him do you want to make a deal?

   Chorus:
   How does it feel
   How does it feel
   To be on your own
   With no direction home
   Like a complete unknown
   Like a rolling stone?

3. You never turned around to see the frowns on the jugglers and the clowns
   When they all come down and do tricks for you
   You never understood that it ain't no good
   You shouldn't let other people get your kicks for you
   You used to ride on the chrome horse with your diplomat
   Who carried on his shoulder a Siamese cat
   Ain't it hard when you discover that
   He really wasn't where it's at
   After he took from you everything he could steal

   Chorus:
   How does it feel
   How does it feel
   To be on your own
   With no direction home
   Like a complete unknown
   Like a rolling stone?

4. Princess on the steeple and all the pretty people
   They're drinkin', thinkin' that they got it made
   Exchanging all kinds of precious gifts and things
   But you'd better lift your diamond ring, you'd better pawn it babe
   You used to be so amused
   At Napoleon in rags and the language that he used
   Go to him now, he calls you, you can't refuse
   When you got nothing, you got nothing to lose
   You're invisible now, you got no secrets to conceal

   Chorus:
   How does it feel
   How does it feel
   To be on your own
   With no direction home
   Like a complete unknown
   Like a rolling stone?

MAGGIE'S FARM
Words and Music by Bob Dylan

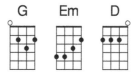

G   Em   D

Medium bright

G

1. I ain't gon - na work on Mag-gie's farm no more
2. - 5. *See additional lyrics*

No, I ain't gon - na work on Mag-gie's

farm no more Well, I

wake in the morn-ing Fold my hands and pray for rain I got a

head full of i - de-as That are driv-in' me in - sane It's a

Em   **D**

shame the way she makes me scrub the floor I

G

ain't gon - na work on Mag-gie's farm no more

(play 5 times)

2. - 5. I

Additional lyrics

2. I ain't gonna work for Maggie's brother no more
   No, I ain't gonna work for Maggie's brother no more
   Well, he hands you a nickel
   He hands you a dime
   He asks you with a grin
   If you're havin' a good time
   Then he fines you every time you slam the door
   I ain't gonna work for Maggie's brother no more

3. I ain't gonna work for Maggie's pa no more
   No, I ain't gonna work for Maggie's pa no more
   Well, he puts his cigar
   Out in your face just for kicks
   His bedroom window
   It is made out of bricks
   The National Guard stands around his door
   Ah, I ain't gonna work for Maggie's pa no more

4. I ain't gonna work for Maggie's ma no more
   No, I ain't gonna work for Maggie's ma no more
   Well, she talks to all the servants
   About man and God and law
   Everybody says
   She's the brains behind pa
   She's sixty-eight, but she says she's twenty-four
   I ain't gonna work for Maggie's ma no more

5. I ain't gonna work on Maggie's farm no more
   No, I ain't gonna work on Maggie's farm no more
   Well, I try my best
   To be just like I am
   But everybody wants you
   To be just like them
   They sing while you slave and I just get bored
   I ain't gonna work on Maggie's farm no more

MR. TAMBOURINE MAN
Words and Music by Bob Dylan

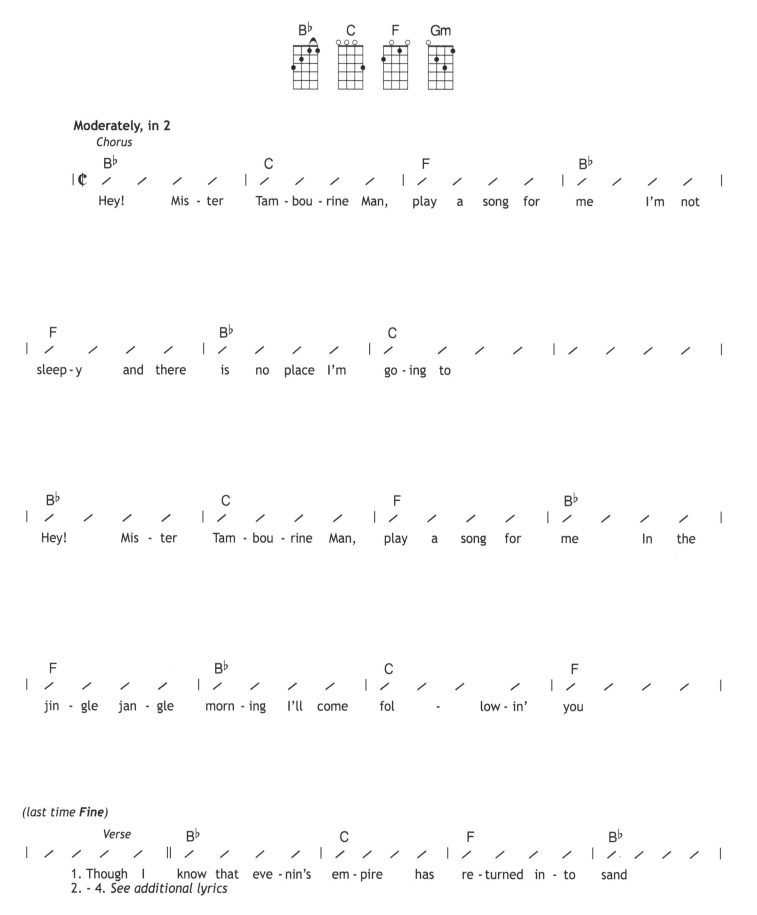

Moderately, in 2

Chorus

Hey! Mis - ter Tam - bou - rine Man, play a song for me   I'm not

sleep - y   and there is no place I'm go - ing to

Hey! Mis - ter Tam - bou - rine Man, play a song for me   In the

jin - gle jan - gle morn - ing I'll come fol - low - in' you

*(last time **Fine**)*

Verse

1. Though I know that eve - nin's em - pire has re - turned in - to sand
2. - 4. *See additional lyrics*

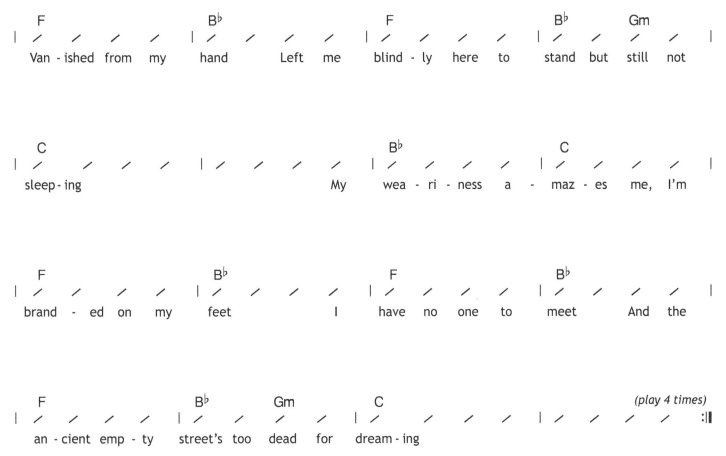

F   Bb   F   Bb   Gm

Van - ished from my hand   Left me blind - ly here to stand but still not

C   Bb   C

sleep - ing   My wea - ri - ness a - maz - es me, I'm

F   Bb   F   Bb

brand - ed on my feet   I have no one to meet   And the

F   Bb   Gm   C   *(play 4 times)*

an - cient emp - ty street's too dead for dream - ing

Additional lyrics

2. Take me on a trip upon your magic swirlin' ship
   My senses have been stripped, my hands can't feel to grip
   My toes too numb to step
   Wait only for my boot heels to be wanderin'
   I'm ready to go anywhere, I'm ready for to fade
   Into my own parade, cast your dancing spell my way
   I promise to go under it

3. Though you might hear laughin', spinnin', swingin'
     madly across the sun
   It's not aimed at anyone, it's just escapin' on the run
   And but for the sky there are no fences facin'
   And if you hear vague traces of skippin' reels of rhyme
   To your tambourine in time, it's just a ragged clown behind
   I wouldn't pay it any mind
   It's just a shadow you're seein' that he's chasin'

4. Then take me disappearin' through the
     smoke rings of my mind
   Down the foggy ruins of time, far past the frozen leaves
   The haunted, frightened trees, out to the windy beach
   Far from the twisted reach of crazy sorrow
   Yes, to dance beneath the diamond sky with one hand
     wavin' free
   Silhouetted by the sea, circled by the circus sands
   With all memory and fate driven deep beneath the waves
   Let me forget about today until tomorrow

Chorus:
   Hey! Mr. Tambourine Man, play a song for me
   I'm not sleepy and there is no place I'm going to
   Hey! Mr. Tambourine Man, play a song for me
   In the jingle jangle morning I'll come followin' you

Chorus:
   Hey! Mr. Tambourine Man, play a song for me
   I'm not sleepy and there is no place I'm going to
   Hey! Mr. Tambourine Man, play a song for me
   In the jingle jangle morning I'll come followin' you

Chorus:
   Hey! Mr. Tambourine Man, play a song for me
   I'm not sleepy and there is no place I'm going to
   Hey! Mr. Tambourine Man, play a song for me
   In the jingle jangle morning I'll come followin' you

RAINY DAY WOMEN #12 & 35

Words and Music by Bob Dylan

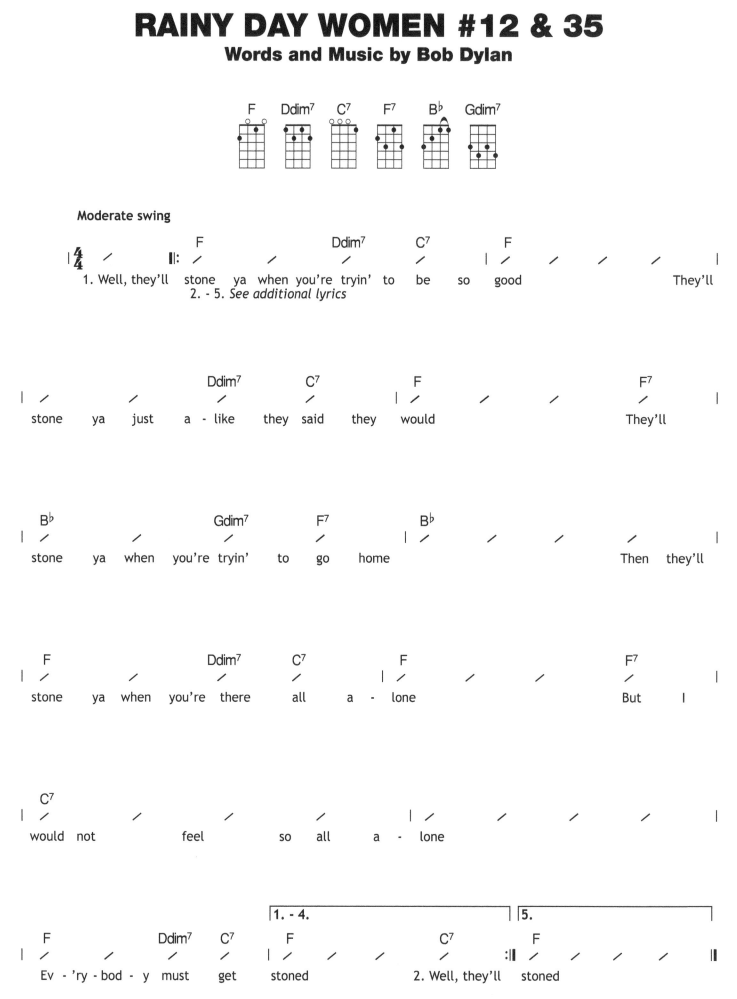

Additional lyrics

2. Well, they'll stone ya when you're walkin' 'long the street
   They'll stone ya when you're tryin' to keep your seat
   They'll stone ya when you're walkin' on the floor
   They'll stone ya when you're walkin' to the door
   But I would not feel so all alone
   Everybody must get stoned

3. They'll stone ya when you're at the breakfast table
   They'll stone ya when you are young and able
   They'll stone ya when you're tryin' to make a buck
   They'll stone ya and then they'll say, "good luck"
   Tell ya what, I would not feel so all alone
   Everybody must get stoned

4. Well, they'll stone you and say that it's the end
   Then they'll stone you and then they'll come back again
   They'll stone you when you're riding in your car
   They'll stone you when you're playing your guitar
   Yes, but I would not feel so all alone
   Everybody must get stoned

5. Well, they'll stone you when you walk all alone
   They'll stone you when you are walking home
   They'll stone you and then say you are brave
   They'll stone you when you are set down in your grave
   But I would not feel so all alone
   Everybody must get stoned

SOMEDAY BABY
Words and Music by Bob Dylan

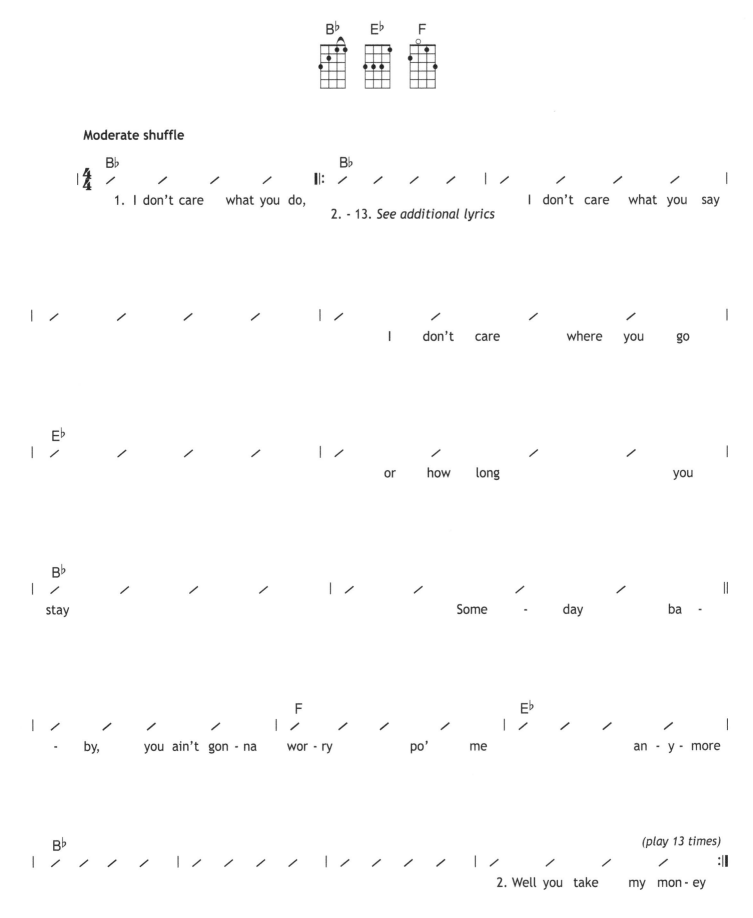

Moderate shuffle

1. I don't care   what you do,
2. - 13. *See additional lyrics*   I don't care   what you say

I   don't   care   where   you   go

or   how   long   you

stay   Some - day   ba -

- by,   you ain't gon - na   wor - ry   po'   me   an - y - more

(play 13 times)

2. Well you take   my mon - ey

Additional lyrics

2. Well you take my money and you turn me out
You fill me up with nothin' but self-doubt
Someday baby, you ain't gonna worry po' me anymore

3. When I was young, driving was my crave
You drive me so hard, almost to the grave
Someday baby, you ain't gonna worry po' me anymore

4. *Instrumental*

5. I'm so hard pressed, my mind tied up in knots
I keep recycling the same old thoughts
Someday baby, you ain't gonna worry po' me anymore

6. So many good things in life that I overlooked
I don't know what to do now, you got me so hooked
Someday baby, you ain't gonna worry po' me anymore

7. *Instrumental*

8. Well, I don't want to brag, but I'm gonna ring your neck
When all else fails I'll make it a matter of self-respect
Someday baby, you ain't gonna worry po' me anymore

9. *Instrumental*

10. You can take your clothes put 'm in a sack
You goin' down the road, baby and you can't come back
Someday baby, you ain't gonna worry po' me anymore

11. I try to be friendly, I try to be kind
Now I'm gonna drive you from your home, just like I was driven from mine
Someday baby, you ain't gonna worry po' me anymore

12. Living this way ain't a natural thing to do
Why was I born to love you?
Someday baby, you ain't gonna worry po' me anymore

13. *Instrumental (fade)*

THE TIMES THEY ARE A-CHANGIN'
Words and Music by Bob Dylan

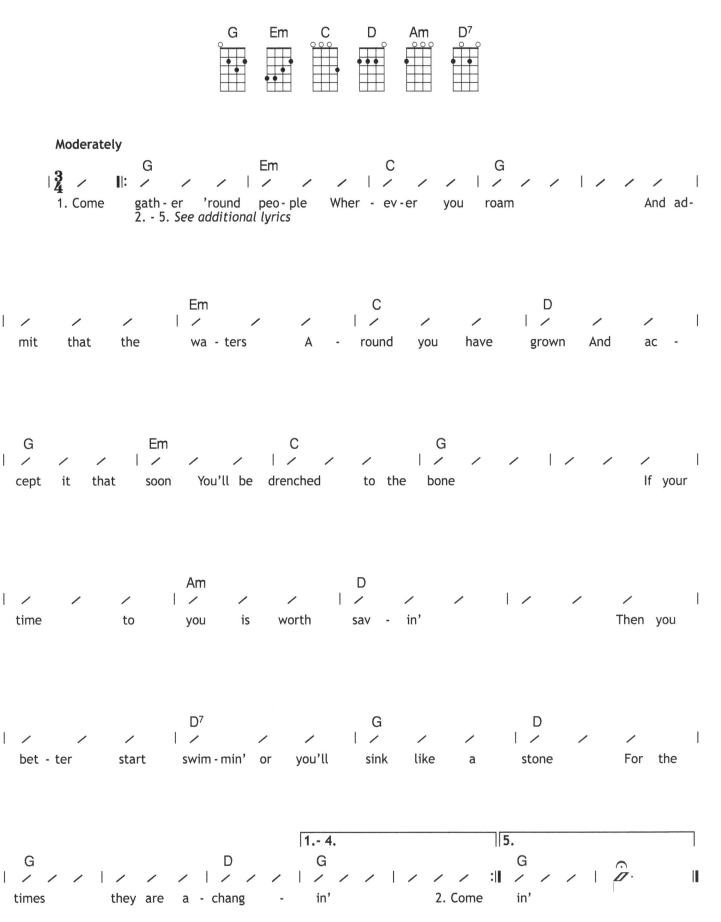

Moderately

1. Come gath-er 'round peo-ple Wher-ev-er you roam And ad-
2. - 5. *See additional lyrics*

mit that the wa-ters A-round you have grown And ac-

cept it that soon You'll be drenched to the bone If your

time to you is worth sav-in' Then you

bet-ter start swim-min' or you'll sink like a stone For the

times they are a-chang-in' 2. Come in'

Additional lyrics

2. Come writers and critics
   Who prophesize with your pen
   And keep your eyes wide
   The chance won't come again
   And don't speak too soon
   For the wheel's still in spin
   And there's no tellin' who that it's namin'
   For the loser now will be later to win
   For the times they are a-changin'

3. Come senators, congressmen
   Please heed the call
   Don't stand in the doorway
   Don't block up the hall
   For he that gets hurt
   Will be he who has stalled
   There's a battle outside and it is ragin'
   It'll soon shake your windows and rattle your walls
   For the times they are a-changin'

4. Come mothers and fathers
   Throughout the land
   And don't criticize
   What you can't understand
   Your sons and your daughters
   Are beyond your command
   Your old road is rapidly agin'
   Please get out of the new one if you can't lend your hand
   For the times they are a-changin'

5. The line it is drawn
   The curse it is cast
   The slow one now
   Will later be fast
   As the present now
   Will later be past
   The order is rapidly fadin'
   And the first one now will later be last
   For the times they are a-changin'

WHEN THE DEAL GOES DOWN
Words and Music by Bob Dylan

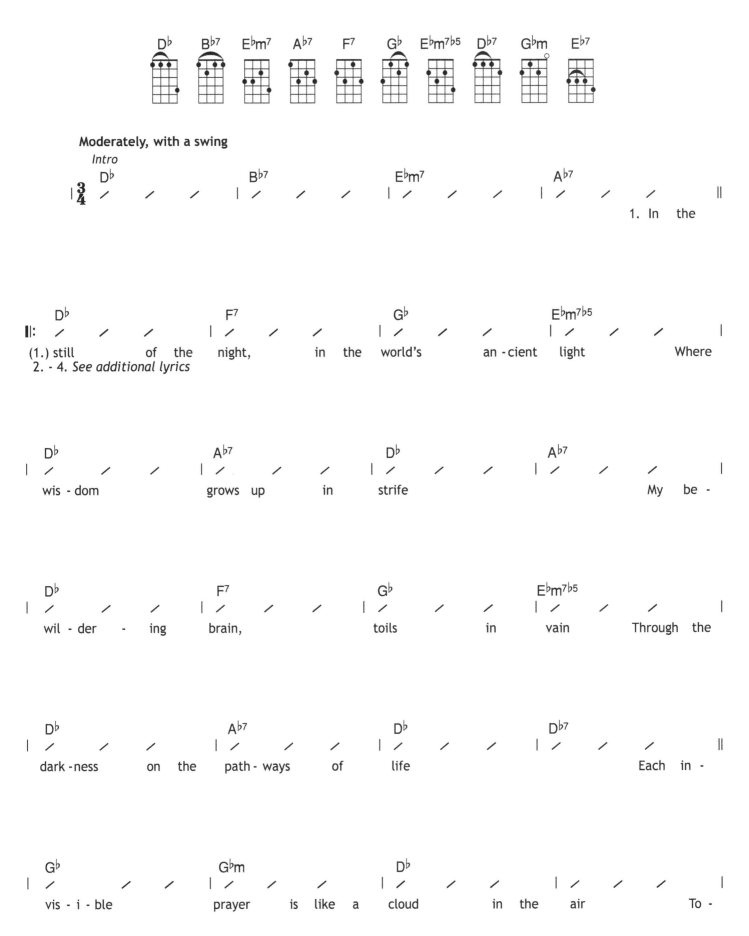

Moderately, with a swing

Intro

Db / / / | **Bb7** / / / | **Ebm7** / / / | **Ab7** / / / ‖

                                      1. In the

‖: **Db** / / / | **F7** / / / | **Gb** / / / | **Ebm7b5** / / / |

(1.) still   of the   night,   in the world's   an - cient light   Where

2. - 4. *See additional lyrics*

Db / / / | **Ab7** / / / | **Db** / / / | **Ab7** / / / |

wis - dom   grows up   in strife   My be -

Db / / / | **F7** / / / | **Gb** / / / | **Ebm7b5** / / / |

wil - der - ing brain,   toils   in vain   Through the

Db / / / | **Ab7** / / / | **Db** / / / | **Db7** / / / ‖

dark -ness   on the path - ways   of   life   Each in -

Gb / / / | **Gbm** / / / | **Db** / / / |

vis - i - ble   prayer is like a cloud   in the air   To -

G♭			D♭			E♭7			A♭7			‖
mor - row	keeps	turn - ing	a	-	round					We

D♭			F7			G♭			E♭m7♭5			
live	and we	die,	we	know not		why	But	I'll be

1. - 3.

D♭			A♭7			D♭			A♭7			:‖
with you	when the	deal	goes	down					2. We

4.

A♭7			D♭			G♭7			E♭m7			E♭m7♭5			D♭			‖
																		rit.	

Additional lyrics

2. We eat and we drink, we feel and we think
   Far down the street we stray
   I laugh and I cry and I'm haunted by
   Things I never meant nor wished to say
   The midnight rain follows the train
   We all wear the same thorny crown
   Soul to soul, our shadows roll
   And I'll be with you when the deal goes down

3. The moon gives light and shines by night
   I scarcely feel the glow
   We learn to live and then we forgive
   O'er the road we're bound to go
   More frailer than the flowers, these precious hours
   That keep us so tightly bound
   You come to my eyes like a vision from the skies
   And I'll be with you when the deal goes down

4. I picked up a rose and it poked through my clothes
   I followed the winding stream
   I heard a deafening noise, I felt transient joys
   I know they're not what they seem
   In this earthly domain, full of disappointment and pain
   You'll never see me frown
   I owe my heart to you, and that's sayin' it true
   And I'll be with you when the deal goes down

YOU AIN'T GOIN' NOWHERE
Words and Music by Bob Dylan

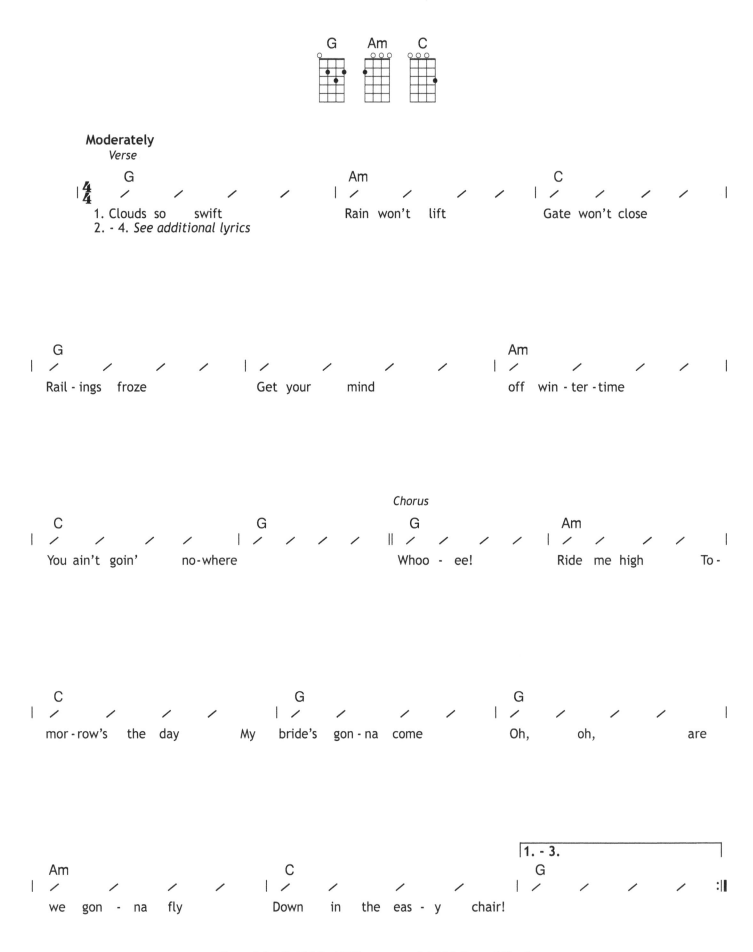

4.

Chorus

G   /   /   /   ‖: G   /   /   /   Am   /   /   /

Whoo - ee!   Ride   me   high   To -

C   /   /   /   G   /   /   /   G   /   /   /

mor - row's   the   day   my   bride's gon - na come   Oh,   oh,   are

(repeat and fade)

Am   /   /   /   C   /   /   /   G   /   /   /   :‖

we   gon - na   fly   Down   in   the   eas - y   chair!

Additional lyrics

2. I don't care
   How many letters they sent
   Morning came and morning went
   Pick up your money
   And pack up your tent
   You ain't goin' nowhere

Chorus
   Whoo-ee! Ride me high
   Tomorrow's the day
   My bride's gonna come
   Oh, oh, are we gonna fly
   Down in the easy chair!

3. Buy me a flute
   And a gun that shoots
   Tailgates and substitues
   Strap yourself
   To the tree with roots
   You ain't goin' nowhere

Chorus
   Whoo-ee! Ride me high
   Tomorrow's the day
   My bride's gonna come
   Oh, oh, are we gonna fly
   Down in the easy chair!

4. Genghis Khan
   He could not keep
   All his kings
   Supplied with sleep
   We'll climb that hill no matter how steep
   When we get up to it

Chorus
   Whoo-ee! Ride me high
   Tomorrow's the day
   My bride's gonna come
   Oh, oh, are we gonna fly
   Down in the easy chair!

UKULELE CHORD CHART

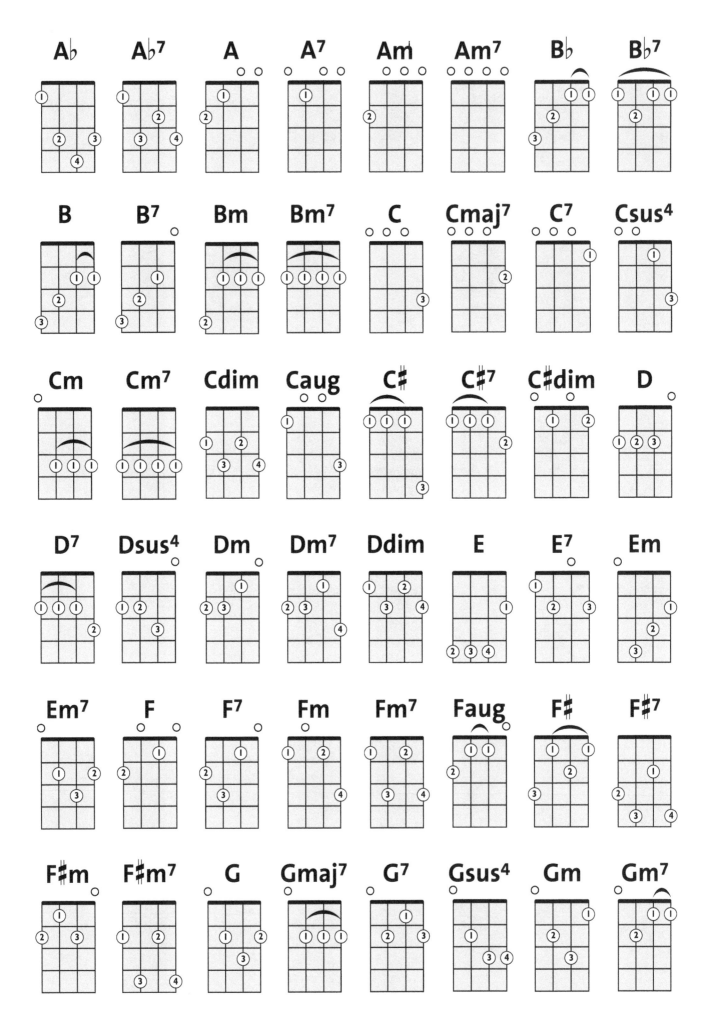